Other books by Ruskin Bond

The Rupa Book of Shikar Stories
The Rupa Book of Nightmare Tales
The Rupa Book of Great Crime Stories
The Rupa Book of Travellers' Tales
The Rupa Book of Haunted Houses
The Rupa Laughter Omnibus
The Rupa Book of Scary Stories
The Rupa Book of Great Suspense Stories
Ghost Stories from the Raj
The Rupa Book of Great Animal Stories
The Rupa Book of True Tales of Mystery and Adventure
The Rupa Book of Ruskin Bond's Himalayan Tales
Ruskin Bond's Children's Omnibus
Angry River
Hanuman to the Rescue
A Long Walk for Bina
The Blue Umbrella
Strange Men, Strange Places
The Road to the Bazaar
Tales and Legends from India
The India I Love
The Ruskin Bond Omnibus-I
The Ruskin Bond Omnibus-II
The Ruskin Bond Omnibus-III
The Rupa Book of Love Stories
The Rupa Book of Indian Love Stories

a little night music

Ruskin Bond

Rupa & Co

Copyright © Ruskin Bond 2004

Published 2004 by
Rupa & Co
7/16, Ansari Road, Daryaganj,
New Delhi 110 002

Sales Centres:
Allahabad Bangalore Chandigarh Chennai
Hyderabad Jaipur Kathmandu
Kolkata Mumbai Pune

All rights reserved.
No part of this publication may be reproduced, stored
in a retrieval system, or transmitted, in any form or
by any means, electronic, mechanical, photocopying, recording
or otherwise, without the prior permission of the publishers.

Typeset in 12 pts. Simoncini Garamond by
Nikita Overseas Pvt Ltd,
1410 Chiranjiv Tower,
43 Nehru Place,
New Delhi 110 019

Printed in India by
Rekha Printers Pvt Ltd,
A-102/1 Okhla Industrial Area, Phase-II
New Delhi 110 020

*For the grandchildren
Siddharth, Shrishti and Gautam*

contents

Foreword ix

Don't Be Afraid of the Dark 1
Look for the Colours of Life 3
Remember the Old Road 5
All Is Life 7
A Plea for Bowlers 9
Butterfly Time 11
Dandelion 12
The Last Flower 13
To the Indian Foresters 14
Night Thoughts 15
In This Workaday World 16
Love's Sad Song 17
We Are the Babus 19
This Land Is Mine 20
Phantom Lover 21
Wild Is the Wind 23
Slum Children at Play 25
Do You Believe in Ghosts? 27
We Must Love Someone 28
The Pool 29
Don't Go to War, My Son 31
Love Is a Law 32

A Little Night Music	33
Dare to Dream	35
The Demon Driver	37
Summer Fruit	39
The Message of the Flowers	41
Granny's Proverbs	45
Foot Soldiers	46
Out of the Darkness	47
A Nightmare	49
Lines Written on a Sleepless Night	51
What Can we Give Our Children?	53
The Duck Is Seventy	54

foreword

Every now and then I indulge myself with a little poetry or light verse—something that I enjoy doing, even if the results are not always published. It is very hard to sell books of poetry, and publishers are naturally reluctant to take them on. Over the years, I have slipped my poems into collections of stories and essays—one way of getting them published!

For a couple of months last summer, I gave myself up to this favourite pastime of mine, and wrote the verses—all new—that appear in this slim volume. Some of the poems are for children; others for older readers.

I enjoyed writing every one of them, and I hope that enjoyment will prove infectious, and that you, dear reader, will derive some pleasure from them too.

Ruskin Bond
August 1, 2004

don't be afraid of the dark

Don't be afraid of the dark, little one,
The earth must rest when the day is done.
The sun may be harsh, but moonlight — never!
And those stars will be shining forever and ever,
Be friends with the Night, there is nothing to fear,
Just let your thoughts travel to friends far and near.
By day, it does seem that our troubles won't cease,
But at night, late at night, the world is at peace.

RUSKIN BOND

look for the colours of life

Colours are everywhere,
Bright blue the sky,
Dark green the forest
And light the fresh grass;
Bright yellow the lights
From a train sweeping past,
The Flame trees glow
At this time of year,
The mangoes burn bright
As the monsoon draws near.

A favourite colour of mine
Is the pink of the candy-floss man
As he comes down the dusty road,
Calling his wares;
And the balloon-man soon follows,
Selling his floating bright colours.

It's early summer
And the roses blush
In the dew-drenched dawn,
And poppies sway red and white
In the invisible breeze.
Only the wind has no colour:

A LITTLE NIGHT MUSIC

But if you look carefully
You will see it teasing
The colour out of the leaves.
And the rain has no colour
But it turns the bronzed grass
To emerald green,
And gives a golden sheen
To the drenched sunflower.
Look for the colours of life—
They are everywhere,
Even in your dreams.

RUSKIN BOND

remember the old road

Remember the old road,
The steep stony path
That took us up from Rajpur,
Toiling and sweating
And grumbling at the climb,
But enjoying it all the same.
At first the hills were hot and bare,
But then there were trees near Jharipani
And we stopped at the Halfway House
And swallowed lungfuls of diamond-cut air.
Then onwards, upwards, to the town,
Our appetites to repair!

Well, no one uses the old road any more.
Walking is out of fashion now.
And if you have a car to take you
Swiftly up the motor-road
Why bother to toil up a disused path?
You'd have to be an old romantic like me
To want to take that route again.
But I did it last year,
Pausing and plodding and gasping for air—
Both road and I being a little worse for wear!

But I made it to the top and stopped to rest
And looked down to the valley and the silver stream
Winding its way towards the plains.
And the land stretched out before me, and the years
    fell away,
And I was a boy again,
And the friends of my youth were there beside me,
And nothing had changed.

all is life

Whether by accident or design,
We are here.
Let's make the most of it, my friend.
Make happiness our pursuit,
Spread a little sunshine here and there.
Enjoy the flowers, the breeze,
Rivers, sea, and sky,
Mountains and tall waving trees.
Greet the children passing by,
Talk to the old folk. Be kind, my friend.
Hold on, in times of pain and strife:
Until death comes, all is life.

RUSKIN BOND

a plea for bowlers

Cricket never will be fair
Till bowlers get their rightful share
For toiling in the mid-day sun.
What should be done?
It's simple ——
Make those wickets broader, taller!
That should make it much more fun
For the poor perspiring bowler.

P.S. And in the interests of the game
      The size of the bat remains the same.

RUSKIN BOND

butterfly time

April showers
Bring swarms of butterflies
Streaming across the valley
Seeking sweet nectar.
Yellow, gold, and burning bright,
Red and blue and banded white.
To my eyes they bring delight!
Theirs a long and arduous flight,
Here today and off tomorrow,
Floating on, bright butterflies,
To distant bowers.
For Nature does things in good order:
And birds and butterflies recognize
No man-made border.

dandelion

I think it's an insult
To Nature's generosity
That many call this cheerful flower
A 'common weed'.
How dare they so degrade
A flower divinely made!
Sublimely does it bloom and seed
In sunshine or in shade,
Thriving in wind and rain,
On stony soil
On walls or steps
On strips of waste;
Tough and resilient,
Giving delight
When other flowers are out of sight.
And when its puff-ball comes to fruit
You make a wish and blow it clean away:
'Please make my wish come true,' you say.
And if you're kind and pure of heart,
Who knows? This magic flower might just respond
And help you on your way.
Good dandelion,
Be mine today.

RUSKIN BOND

the last flower

If, in this dying world,
Only one flower could be left,
Which one would you choose?
The rose, or some sweet violet,
Or would you prefer the fragrant
Mignonette?
Of flowers not yet extinct,
You might just settle for the Indian Pink.
But my first choice, I like to think,
Is the red geranium
Standing on my desk all year,
Far, like a scarlet chanticleer,
It stands up tall
And makes a statement loud and clear.

to the indian foresters

You are the quiet men who do not boast
Although you've done much more than most
To make this land a sea of green
From here to far Cape Comorin.
Without your help to Nature's thrust,
This land would be a bowl of dust.
A land without its forest wealth
Must suffer a decline in health,
For herbs and plants all need green cover
Before they help the sick recover.
And we need trees to hold together
Beasts, and birds of every feather,
And leaves to help the air smell sweet;
All this and more is no mean feat.
Dear foresters, you have not sought for fame or favour,
Yours has been a love of labour.
Our thanks! Instead of desert sand
You've given us this green and growing land.

(Composed and read to a gathering of young forest officers at the Forest Research Institute, on April 10, 2004)

RUSKIN BOND

night thoughts

This mountain is my mother,
My father is the sea,
This river is the fountain
Of all that life may be...
Swift river from the mountain,
Deep river to the sea,
Take all my words and leave them
Where the west wind sets them free.
So, piper on the lonely hill,
Play no sad songs for me;
The day has gone, sweet night comes on,
Its darkness helps me see.

in this workaday world

It's a busy world, I know,
And we must hurry here and there
And not ask who or why or where,
For fear our credits fall too low.
But here upon this hilly crest
There's some respite; and when
The fretting day is done,
Beneath the cherry tree there's rest.

love's sad song

There's a sweet little girl lives down the lane,
And she's so pretty and I'm so plain,
She's clever and smart and all things good,
And I'm the bad boy of the neighbourhood.
But I'd be her best friend forever and a day
If only she'd smile and look my way.

we are the babus

Soak the rich and harry the poor,
That's our motto and our law;
We are the rulers of this land,
We are the *babus*, a merry band,
Under the table, or through the back door,
We'll empty your pockets and ask for more!
We are the *babus*, this is our law—
Soak the rich and harry the poor!

this land is mine

This land is mine
Although I do not own it,
This land is mine
Because I grew upon it.
This dust, this grass,
This tender leaf
And weathered bark
All in my heart are finely blended
Until my time on earth is ended.

RUSKIN BOND

phantom lover

Night unto night
When the world's asleep,
You come to me,
Our tryst to keep.
Held captive, in thrall,
As the stars look down,
Body and soul
From night unto dawn.
Silent you come
And softly you go,
Ours is a love
That none must know.

RUSKIN BOND

wild is the wind

Wild is the wind tonight,
Deep is the thunder,
Lightning across the sky
Splits it asunder.
Witches will ride tonight,
Ranging the sky,
Wizards will cast their spells—
Great men will die.
Who'll be my guide tonight,
Starless the sky;
Who'll brave the demons
Now riding so high.
I'll take the road alone,
I'll reach my goal;
Witches and wizards
Must yield to man's soul.

RUSKIN BOND

slum children at play

Imps of mischief,
Barefoot in the dust,
Grinning, mocking, even as
They beg you for a crust.
No angels these,
Just hungry eyes
And eager hands
To help you sympathise…
They don't want love,
They don't seek pity,
They know there's nothing
In this heartless city
But a kindred need
In those who strive
For power and pelf
Though only just alive!
They know your guilt,
They'll take your money,
And if you give too much
They'll find you funny.
Because that's what you are—

(Delhi, May 1, 2004)

You're just a joke—
Your life is soft
And theirs all grime and smoke.
And yet they shout and sing
And do not thank your giving,
You'll fuss and fret through life
While they do all the living.

do you believe in ghosts?

'Do you believe in ghosts?'
Asked the passenger
On platform number three.
'I'm a rational man,' said I,
'I believe in what I can see—
Your hands, your feet, your beard!'
'Then look again,' said he,
And promptly disappeared!

we must love someone

We must love someone
If we are to justify
Our presence on this earth.
We must keep loving all our days,
Someone, anyone, anywhere
Outside our selves;
For even the sarus crane
Will grieve over its lost companion,
And the seal its mate.
Somewhere in life
There must be someone
To take your hand
And share the torrid day.
Without the touch of love
There is no life, and we must fade away.

RUSKIN BOND

the pool

Where has it gone,
            the pool on the hill?
The pool of our youth,
            when Time stood still,
Where we romped in its shallows
            and wrestled on sand,
Closer than brothers, a colourful band.

Gone is the pool, now filled in with rocks,
Having made way for the builders' blocks.
But sometimes, at dawn,
            you will hear us still,
And that's why they call this
            the Haunted Hill.

don't go to war, my son

Blood drying in the fierce sun
Vultures feasting on the dead
Mangled limbs and severed heads
Battles lost or battles won
Must end in madness when they're done.
Don't go to war, my son.

love is a law

Who shall set a law to lovers?
Love is a law unto itself

Love gained is often lost
And love that's lost is found again

It's love that makes the world go round
Love that keeps us closely bound

Take this power to love away
We would be just beasts of prey

If Love should lose its hold on us
Discord would rule the Universe.

RUSKIN BOND

a little night music

Open the window
Let in the Night
All that is lovely
Comes at this hour
Moonlight and moonbeam
And fragrance of flower
Blossoming Champa
And Queen of the Night—
And sometimes a field mouse
Drops in for a bite.
High in the tree-tops
An owl strikes a note
And the frogs in their pond
Sing out as they float
Along on their lily-pads...
The Brain-fever bird
Is calling on high
'Brain fever, brain fever!'
Its monotonous cry.
The Nightjar plays trombone
The crickets join in
An out-of-tune orchestra
Making a din!
I lie awake listening

To the wild duck in flight
As they fly to the north
For their annual respite;
And a star in the heavens
Sweeps past as it falls,
A leopard's out hunting—
The swamp deer calls.
A breeze has spring up,
It hums in the trees
The window is rattling
And I must cease
From my Nocturne
And shut out the Night.

Goodnight, birds
Goodnight, frogs
Goodnight, stars
Goodnight sweet Night.

dare to dream

Build castles in the air
But first, give them foundations.
Hold fast to all your dreams,
Make perfect your creations.

All glory comes to those who dare.

Failed works are sad lame things.
Act impeccably, sing
Your own song, but do not take
Another's song from her or him;
Look for your art within,
You'll find your own true gift,
For you are special too.
And if you try, you'll find
There's nothing you can't do.

the demon driver

At driving a car I've never been good—
I batter the bumper and damage the hood—
'Get off the road!' the traffic cops shout,
'You're supposed to go *round* that roundabout!'
'I thought it was quicker to drive straight through.'
'Give us your license — it's time to renew.'
I took their advice and handed a fee
To a Babu who looked on this windfall with glee.
'No problem,' he said, 'Your license now pukka,
You may drive all the way from here to Kolkata.'

So away I drove, at a feverish pitch,
Advancing someway down an unseen ditch.
Once back on the highway, I soon joined the fray
Of hundreds of drivers who wouldn't give way:
I skimmed past a truck and revolved round a van
(Good drivers can do anything that they can)
Then offered a lift to a man with a load—
'Just a little way down to the end of this road,'
As I pressed on the pedal, the car gave a shudder:
He'd got in at one door, got out at the other.
'God help you!' he said, as he hurried away,
'I'll come for a drive another fine day!'
I came to that roundabout, round it I sped

Eager to get to my dinner and bed.
Round it I went, and round it once more
'Get off the road!' That cop was a bore.
I swung to the left and went clean through a wall,
My neighbour stood there — he looked menacing,
    tall—
'This will cost you three thousand,' he quietly said,
'And send me your cheque before you're in bed!'

Alas! my new car was sent for repair,
But my friends gathered round and said, never despair!
'We are all going to help you to make a fresh start.'
And next day they gave me a nice bullock-cart.

summer fruit

Summer is here, and mangoes too
And fruit of every taste and hue;
And given a choice of juice or berry,
I'll settle for the humble cherry.
I know *your* favourite on this planet
Is the red and rosy pomegranate;
But that's a winter fruit, my child,
So wait until the weather's mild.
But if you like a simple khana,
There's nothing like a good banana.
No? Something more exotic?
Maybe some lichis in your pockets.
Or would you like a large tarbuj—
Its sweeter than a good kharbuj—
Tarbuj, kharbuja — oh, what's the difference?
Tell me, children, and your preference

the message of the flowers

Apple Blossom	It's Spring, and apple blossom time Stands for temptation, Give in to it!
Bluebells	Stand for constancy and calm. For troubled souls they act as balm Ring out the old, ring in the new!
Carnation	Ah, a woman's love comes with this flower. Cherish the moment!
Crysanthemum	When red, it's love. When white, it's youth. When bronze, it has the ring of truth.
Cornflower	How delicate you are!
Daisy	The power of innocence.
Daffodils	You purify the air. You're chivalry, gratitude and care.
Eglantine	Sweet brier-rose, the flower of poets. Keats called you rain-scented, dew-sweet.

Forget-me-not	Your name says it all. And I'll remember to remember.
Geranium	Especially the scarlet kind, They say scarlet is a sign of folly. In that case, you're my folly.
Honeysuckle	Who can resist your sweet fragrance? I want to be near you.
Ivy	You are friendship, fellowship and fidelity You stand for permanence.
Jasmine	Flower of perfection, You stand high in my affection.
Lemon Blossom	What made me think of you today? You stir up memories of love and play.
Magnolia	Champa, Queen of the garden You bring good fortune.
Nasturtium	How can I forget you, humble friend? You gladden my heart to winter's end.
Oleander	Red or white You're the poet's delight.

RUSKIN BOND

Poppy	You're my scarlet lady— Extravagant, effervescent, evanescent!
Quercus	Q had me in a quandary Until I looked out of my window And saw my old friend the oak tree staring hard at me!
Roses	Of roses there are many kinds— The moss, the musk, the Eglantine; Roses speak of faithfulness, The red rose of voluptuousness.
Snapdragon	Your sweet scent fills the air and draws me to you; I'd follow you anywhere.

Tulips	I was offered a tulip, they said it
	   stood for fame
	I'll settle for the Thorn-Apple, if to
	   you it's just the same.

Urtica	The common nettle: You ignore it at your peril!
Violet	Modest and sweet— I look for you in quiet corners.

A LITTLE NIGHT MUSIC

Wallflower	Wallflower bright against my wall, You are the sturdiest flower of all!
Xerophyte	You thought you'd fool me, Mr. X I looked you up, I must confess In the desert you exist Where other plants like you persist...
Yellow Iris	You speak of passion — love's dream ends.
Zinnia	You bring me thoughts of absent friends.

granny's proverbs

A hungry man is an angry man,
    Said dear old Gran
As she prepared an Irish stew
For the chosen few
(Gran'dad, my cousins and me).
But then she'd turn to me and emote—
'Don't be greedy, or your tongue will cut your throat!'
And if I asked for more of my favourite fish,
'That small fish,' she'd say, 'is better than
                              an empty dish!'
Like Mann, she taught us to honour our food,
She was the law-giver, seeking all good.
Gran'dad and I, we'd eat what we were given
    (Irish stew and a tart)
But sometimes we'd sneak away to the bazaar
To feast on tikkees and chaat
    —And that was heaven!

(You can read more about my grandparents in 'Grandfather's Private Zoo' in my children's omnibus.)

A LITTLE NIGHT MUSIC

foot soldiers

'Where's Solan?' the private was asking.
'Somewhere in Tibet, I should think.'
'There's a brewery there,
And it's brimming with beer,
But we can't get a mouthful to drink!'

So we route-march from Delhi to Solan
In the dust and the devilish sun,
And we're cursing away like Hades,
'Cause there ain't any ladies
To hear every son-of-a-gun!

And when we have climbed up to Solan
Our language continues profane,
For right well we know
We shall soon have to go.
Down from Solan to Delhi again.

(Based on an old ditty my soldier-grandfather used to sing. The Solan Brewery is 150 years old.)

RUSKIN BOND

out of the darkness

Out of darkness we came, into darkness we go,
Out of the sea to the land we know,
Out of the trembling hills and its streams,
From night unto day we come with our dreams.

The wind and the water gave form to our lives;
After thousands of aeons mankind still survives,
And beyond those great spaces, those planets and stars,
Who knows, there are heart-beats and children like ours.

a nightmare

Cupid, with his famous dart,
Struck me just above the heart—
'Life' he said, 'is just a gamble,
You'll take to her without preamble.
And so there came, all bent and grey,
This withered crone, and she did sway
Backwards and forwards, as though she'd seen
The phantom lover of a dream.
She hypnotised me with one glance
And there and then began to dance,
Then tossed me in her waiting carriage
And promised me her hand in marriage.
She took me to her home in state,
And chortling, said, 'There's no escape,
I'll keep you in my empty cupboard;
You know my name — it's Mother Hubbard!
I'll feed you frogs and make you fat—
A *kofta* for my favourite cat.'
Her cat? The thing she called her darling
Was a monstrous tiger, fiercely snarling,
Its eyes were burning bright and red.
    It pounced! I woke up in my bed.
No tiger lady in my cupboard...

But when I opened my front door
I found the brass plate bore
My name: Mr. Hubbard.

lines written on a sleepless night

I'm unfamiliar with statistics,
I wouldn't know what to do
With a book on Mathematics
Or a girl of ninety-two.

I really can't tell the difference
Between a man from Kalamazoo*
And the kind of endangered species
That you only find in a zoo.

I'm hopeless at Nuclear Physics—
Don't ask me to make you a bomb—
But if you would like me to bake you a cake,
I'll do it with great aplomb.

I'm not very good at book-keeping,
My accounting, they say, is too lax.
I can't trace my Income, or, credit my debit,
So how can I pay Income Tax?

I'm really not bad at prognosis,
Consult me — I won't take a fee—
I'll soon let you know if your calcium is low
Or if it's just Housemaid's Knee.

---

* There is such a place — or used to be.

I'm not very good with a Nurse
And I feel more at ease writing verse—
I'm inclined to convulse when she feels for my pulse,
And if I feel *hers*, she gets terse!

I'm hopeless at counting those sheep—
I'd rather be off with Bo-Peep!
If she'd leave them alone
And take me straight home
I wouldn't mind losing more sleep.

On the night before my 70th Birthday, I just couldn't sleep. Whenever I was on the verge of dozing off, one of these silly verses would pop into my head. On each occasion I'd get up, put it down on paper, and go back to bed. It might have been better if I'd forgotten them. On the other hand, Gautam says publish and be damned.

RUSKIN BOND

what can we give our children?

What can we give our children?
Knowledge, yes, and honour too,
And strength of character
And the gift of laughter.
What gold do we give our children?
The gold of a sunny childhood,
Open spaces, a home that binds
Us to the common good...
These simple things
Are greater than the gold of kings.

A LITTLE NIGHT MUSIC

the duck is seventy

This year, '04, I'm 70 years old,
And so is Donald Duck, I'm told.
At writing verse he's rather slack,
I'm not much better when I quack!
So here, dear Donald, is my boast—
Roast duck is best with buttered toast.
Says Donald, 'Friend, don't push your luck,
You might be born again a duck!'

(For Shubhadarshini)

*In the sways of Winter
Out in the ~~frosty day~~ cold December,
The wind has started to shake
Snow falls down from head to toe
As the children begin to ponder

The birds sing a song yet to come
Why don't you come out and have some fun?*

RUSKIN BOND